GREAT CONDUCTORS
In Historic Photographs

---

193 Portraits from 1860 to 1960

Edited by
James Camner

DOVER PUBLICATIONS, INC.
NEW YORK

Editor and publisher are grateful to Mr. Lim M. Lai for lending the following photos: frontispiece, 2, 4, 6, 10, 12, 18, 22, 25, 27, 28, 29, 30, 31, 36, 37, 38, 39, 40, 41, 46, 47, 49, 50, 55, 56, 63, 64, 67, 69, 70, 76, 78, 79, 80, 82, 83, 85, 88, 90, 91, 93, 94, 98, 101, 102, 103, 106, 108, 109, 112, 116, 121, 124, 125, 129, 134, 135, 136, 138, 141, 142, 143, 144, 145, 148, 152, 159, 160, 161, 167, 169, 171, 176, 179, 180, 181, 182, 183, 184, 186, 190.

The other photos are from private collections and the files of La Scala Autographs, Inc.

No. 129 courtesy of Mrs. Jonel Perlea.

FRONTISPIECE: **Rafael Kubelík** (born 1914), Swiss conductor of Czech birth (son of the great violinist Jan Kubelík). Conductor of the Czech Philharmonic (Prague), 1941–48; the Chicago Symphony, 1950–53; Covent Garden orchestra, 1955–58; the Bavarian Radio Symphony (Munich) from 1961. Also international guest conductor; in the photo he is leading the Concertgebouw Orchestra (Amsterdam). (Photo: Maria Austria of Particam Pictures; Netherlands Information Service.)

Published in Canada by General Publishing Company, Ltd., 30 Lesmill Road, Don Mills, Toronto, Ontario.
Published in the United Kingdom by Constable and Company, Ltd., 10 Orange Street, London WC2H 7EG.

Great Conductors in Historic Photographs: 193 Portraits from 1860 to 1960 is a new work, first published by Dover Publications, Inc., in 1982.

Book Design by Paula Goldstein

Manufactured in the United States of America
Dover Publications, Inc.
180 Varick Street
New York, N.Y. 10014

Library of Congress Cataloging in Publication Data
Main entry under title:

Great conductors in historic photographs.

1. Conductors (Music)—Portraits.
2. Music—Pictorial works. I. Camner, James.
ML87.G819   1982   780'.92'2   82-14586
ISBN 0-486-24397-4

FOREWORD

The advent of the virtuoso conductor as a dominant force in music making coincided with the dawn of the age of photography. Because of this, *Great Conductors in Historic Photographs* includes most of the important and famous conductors of history.

Beginning with Michael Costa, the first of musicians to gain greater fame for his conducting than for his compositions, and continuing through Nikisch, Toscanini and Furtwängler, this collection of photographs of maestri gives an invaluable insight into the development of a music tradition. The modern symphonic concert was created and built upon by these men; their legacy remains with every symphony orchestra in existence today.

Complementing their many recordings are the portraits of Toscanini, Szell and others, while for such men as Costa and Hans von Bülow these photos remain among our only clues to their impact on an audience. Leopold Stokowski shows us in his photograph the theatrical glamour he cultivated that enhanced his fame as a musician, but the spiritualism of more reticent conductors like Bruno Walter and Felix Weingartner is revealed, as well as the intensity of a Toscanini and the hypnotic power of a Nikisch.

Although many of the giants whose work made their names familiar to symphonic audiences are equally familiar in photographs, many of the portraits are entertainingly untypical. And the pictures of men such as Hermann Levi, the conductor of the first performance of *Parsifal,* and Czech conductor Václav Talich are unusual glimpses of these immortals of the podium.

1. Claudio Abbado (born 1933), Italian conductor. Began conducting in the late 1950s. From 1971, musical director of the La Scala Opera House (Milan) and principal conductor of the Vienna Philharmonic. From 1979, principal conductor of the London Symphony. **2. Ernest Ansermet** (1883–1969), Swiss conductor. Founder of the Orchestre de la Suisse Romande (Geneva), 1918, which he directed until retiring in 1966. Notable interpreter of modern, especially French, composers.

1

2

3. **Hermann Abendroth** (1883–1956), German conductor. After conductorships in Lübeck and Essen, in Cologne for some 20 years from 1914, then director of the Gewandhaus Orchestra (Leipzig) to 1945. Later, conductor of the Weimar Symphony. (Photo: M. Pál Vajda, Budapest.) **4. Karel Ančerl** (1908–1973), Czech conductor. Leader of Czech Philharmonic (Prague), 1950–68. Music director of Toronto Symphony from 1969.

5

6

5. Michael Balling (1866–1925), German conductor. International career, including Bayreuth, Barcelona and Manchester. From 1919, general music director in Darmstadt. (Photo: A. Pieperhoff.) **6. Giuseppe Bamboschek** (1890–1969), American conductor of Italian birth. Conducted at Metropolitan Opera (N.Y.), 1916–29.

7

7. Sir John Barbirolli (1899–1970), English conductor and cellist. Impressive credits include leadership of N.Y. Philharmonic, 1936–42, and of Hallé Orchestra (Manchester) from 1943. Principal conductor of Houston Symphony, 1961–67. Numerous worldwide guest appearances.

8

9

8 & 9. Sir Thomas Beecham (1879–1961), English conductor. Founded his own orchestra in 1909. Important work in opera and ballet during 1910s and 1920s, partly with own opera company. Founded the London Philharmonic in 1932, the year in which he also became artistic director of Covent Garden. Created the Royal Philharmonic in 1946. Has been called "the most gifted executive musician England has ever produced."

11

12

10 & 11. Leonard Bernstein (born 1918, American conductor and composer. Gained fame as assistant conductor of N.Y. Philharmonic in 1944. Head of conducting department at Tanglewood, 1951–55. Back with N.Y. Philharmonic from 1957. Extensive tours, guest appearances, television work. (Photo 10: David Nilsson, 1944.) **12. Howard Barlow** (1892–1972), American conductor. Chiefly known for radio work with CBS Symphony and the Firestone Hour.

13

14

13. Leo Blech (1871–1958), German conductor and composer. Conductor at the German theater in Prague, 1899–1906; then with Berlin Court Opera, 1906–23, and Berlin State Opera, 1926–37. After years in Riga and Stockholm, returned to Berlin in 1949. (Photo: J. Massak, Prague; signed 1905 with quote from Blech's 1903 opera *Alpenkönig und Menschenfeind.*) **14. Artur Bodanzky** (1877–1939), Austrian conductor. At Metropolitan Opera (N.Y.) from 1915 until his death. Also conducted symphonic works. (Photo: Mishkin, N.Y.; signed 1916.)

15

16

15 & 16. Karl Böhm (1894–1981), Austrian conductor. Worked in opera and concert in Graz, Munich, Darmstadt, Hamburg, Dresden and Vienna before free-lancing from 1956. Great interpreter of the Austrian and German classics. (Photo 16: Siegfried Lauterwasser, Überlingen.) **17. Willi Boskovsky** (born 1909), Austrian conductor and violinist. A Strauss-family specialist, he has conducted the Vienna New Year's Day Concerts since 1954 and has led the Vienna Strauss Orchestra since 1969.

17

18

20

19

18. Pierre Boulez (born 1925), French conductor and composer. Began conducting in 1950s. Has been conductor of the Cleveland Orchestra and N.Y. Philharmonic, and has led concerts and operas in many other countries. (Photo: Lotte Meitner-Graf, London, early 1970s.)   **19. Sir Adrian Boult** (born 1889), English conductor. Outstanding, internationally active conductor who led the first performance of Holst's *Planets* (1918) and made the BBC Symphony a major orchestra (from 1930). (Photo: Fayer, Vienna; signed 1933.)   **20. Gustav Brecher** (1879–1940), German conductor. Active in various German cities from 1897 to 1933. (Photo: Dührkoop.)

21

21 & 22. Hans von Bülow (1830–1894), conductor and pianist. One of the nineteenth-century
giants, he conducted the world premieres of both
Tristan und Isolde (1865) and *Die Meistersinger*
(1868) at the Munich Court Opera, and was an
early champion of Brahms and Tchaikovsky.

22

23

23. Guido Cantelli (1920–1956), Italian conductor. A protégé of Toscanini, he was associated with the Philharmonia (London) from 1951 and had just been appointed as principal conductor at La Scala when he died in an air crash.

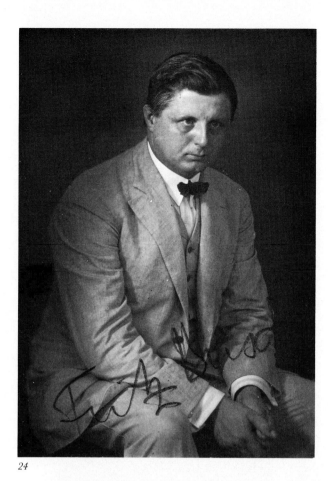

24

24 & 25. Fritz Busch (1890–1951), German conductor and pianist. Music director of the Dresden State Opera, 1922–33, he achieved his greatest fame as conductor of the Glyndebourne Festival, 1934–39 and 1950, establishing a high standard for Mozart interpretation.

25

26

27

26. Cleofonte Campanini (1860–1919), Italian conductor of opera. He led the world premieres of *Adriana Lecouvreur* (1902) and *Madama Butterfly* (1904) at La Scala and the first American performance of *Otello* (1888). From 1906 to 1909 he was with Oscar Hammerstein's Manhattan Opera House, from 1910 with the Chicago Opera. (Photo: Mishkin, N.Y.) **27. Carlos Chávez** (1899–1978), Mexican composer and conductor. First director of the Mexico Symphony, 1928–48, he also made many guest appearances. **28. Fausto Cleva** (1920–1971), American conductor of Italian birth. A pillar of the Metropolitan Opera from 1920 to his death, he was also active in Cincinnati, San Francisco and Chicago. **29. Sergiu Celibidache** (born 1912), Rumanian conductor. Principal conductor of the Berlin Philharmonic, 1945–52; later associated with radio orchestras in Stuttgart and Stockholm. (Photo: London Daily Express, 1964.)

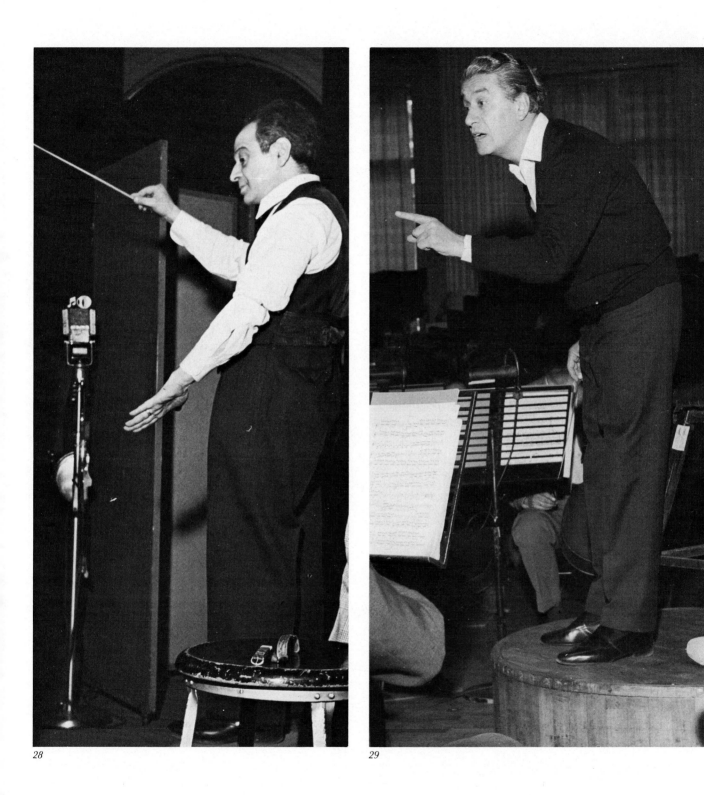

28

29

15

30

30 & 32. Walter Damrosch (1862–1950), American conductor of German birth. Directed his own touring opera company in the U.S., 1894–99; later led the New York Symphony Society. In 1927 became music adviser to NBC Radio. (Photo 30: from the 1939 Paramount film *The Star Maker*. Photo 32: Falk, N.Y.)

31

31. **Edouard Colonne** (1838–1910), French conductor and violinist. Founder of the great Parisian orchestral association the Concerts Colonne, he established Berlioz in public favor. **33. Sir Michael Costa** (1808–1884), English conductor of Italian birth. Eminent conductor of Italian opera in London, 1832–81; of the Philharmonic Society, 1846–54; and of numerous choral festivals.

32

33

34

35

36

34. Issay Dobrowen (1894–1953), Norwegian conductor of Russian birth. Specialist in Russian music in Germany, Hungary and the U.S. before settling in Scandinavian countries and making numerous guest appearances elsewhere. (Photo signed 1933.) **35. Sir Colin Davis** (born 1927), English conductor. Becoming widely known in the late 1950s, he was music director of the Sadler's Wells Opera, 1961–64; principal conductor of the BBC Symphony, 1967–71; and has been music director of Covent Garden since 1971. **36. Albert Coates** (1882–1953), English conductor and composer. Principal conductor at the Mariinsky Theatre (St. Petersburg), 1911–16. Regular conductor of the London Symphony, 1919–23. Music director of the Rochester (N.Y.) Philharmonic, 1923–25.

37. Désiré Defauw (1885–1960), American conductor of Belgian birth. Conducted the concerts of the Brussels Conservatory, 1926–40; led the Chicago Symphony, 1943–47, and the Gary Symphony, 1950–58. (Photo: George Nelidoff, Chicago.) **38. Victor De Sabata** (1892–1967), Italian conductor and composer. Conductor at Monte Carlo Opera, 1918–29, where he led the world premiere of Ravel's *L'enfant et les sortilèges* (1925). With La Scala, 1930–57 (artistic director from 1953).

37

38

39. Antal Dorati (born 1906), American conductor of Hungarian birth. After conducting in Budapest, Dresden and Münster, he led the Ballets Russes de Monte Carlo from 1933 to 1941, then the American Ballet Theater to 1945. From then to 1949 he was with the Dallas Symphony, then 11 years with the Minneapolis Symphony. From 1963 to 1966, principal conductor of the BBC Symphony, then with the Stockholm Philharmonic; important work also in Washington and London. (Photo: Don Berg, Minneapolis.)

40

41

42

40. Arthur Fiedler (1894–1979), American conductor. Director of the Boston Pops from 1930 to his death. **41. Renato Fasano** (born 1902), Italian conductor and composer. Founder-director of I Virtuosi di Roma from 1952. **42. Karl Ellmendorff** (1891–1962), German conductor. Regular conductor at Bayreuth, 1927–42; active in many German cities. (Photo: Franz Grainer, Munich; signed 1926.)

43

44

43. Oskar Fried (1871–1941), German conductor and composer. Led various Berlin orchestras before moving to Tiflis (USSR) as a conductor of opera. (Photo signed Vienna, 1925.) **44. Dirk Foch** (1886–1973), Dutch conductor. Active in Vienna and N.Y. as well as at home. (Photo signed Vienna, 1927.) **45. Grzegorz Fitelberg** (1879–1953), Polish conductor and composer. Connected with the Young Poland in Music movement, he became principal conductor of the Warsaw Philharmonic in 1908. Conducted for Diaghilev, 1921–24; organized and led the Polish Royal Symphony. (Photo signed 1937.)

45

46

46 & 47. Wilhelm Furtwängler (1886–1954), German conductor and composer. Became director of the Lübeck Opera at age 25. In 1922, succeeded Nikisch as conductor of the Gewandhaus (Leipzig) and (especially) the Berlin Philharmonic. Although much hostility was aroused by his decision to remain in Germany during the Third Reich, he is considered by many as one of the supreme conductors of the century. See also no. 82. (Photo 47: Hoenisch, Leipzig.)

47

48

48. Ossip Gabrilovitch (1878–1936), American conductor and pianist of Russian birth. Conducted the Munich Konzertverein, 1910–14, and the Detroit Symphony from 1918. (Photo: Mary Dale Clarke.) **49. Piero Gamba** (born 1937), Italian conductor. Conducted Beethoven's First in Rome at age 8, then toured as prodigy; still active. (Photo: 1947.)

49

50

50. Lamberto Gardelli (born 1915), Swedish conductor of Italian birth. Resident conductor with Swedish Royal Opera, 1946–55, and with the Danish Radio Symphony, 1955–61. Has conducted at the Metropolitan, Glyndebourne and Covent Garden. **51. Wilhelm Gericke** (1845–1925), Austrian conductor and composer. Chiefly active in Vienna, he also led the Boston Symphony, 1884–89 and 1898–1906. (Photo: Marceau, Boston; signed 1906.)

51

52

53

54

52. Vladimir Golschmann (1893–1972), American conductor of French birth. Founded the avant-garde Concerts Golschmann in Paris in 1919; conducted for Diaghilev; led St. Louis Symphony, 1931–56. Later, music director in Tulsa and Denver. **53. Sir Eugene Goossens** (1893–1962), English conductor and composer. Led own orchestra in London, 1921. From 1923 to 1946, conducted Rochester (N.Y.) Philharmonic and was permanent conductor of the Cincinnati Symphony, 1931–46, and resident conductor of the Sydney (Australia) Symphony, 1947–56. (Photo signed Cincinnati, 1936.) **54. Edwin Franko Goldman** (1878–1956), American bandmaster and composer. Formed own band, 1911; began famous outdoor concerts, 1918. (Photo: Harris & Ewing, Washington, D.C.; signed 1932.)

55

55. Morton Gould (born 1913), American conductor and composer. Active in radio, television and films as well as in the concert hall. **56. Carlo Maria Giulini** (born 1914), Italian conductor. Succeeded De Sabata as principal conductor at La Scala, 1953. Associated with Philharmonia Orchestra (London) from 1955. Principal conductor of Vienna Symphony, 1973–76, then moved to Los Angeles.

56

57

59

58

57. Sir Hamilton Harty (1879–1941), Irish conductor and composer. Permanent conductor of the Hallé Orchestra (Manchester), 1920–33; later, active in London. (Photo: Claude Harris, London.) **58. Sir Charles Hallé** (1819–1895), English conductor of German birth. Began conducting at age 11. After activity in Germany and France, he settled in Manchester, in 1849 founding the orchestra that still bears his name and leading it the rest of his life. (Photo: Elliott & Fry, London.) **59. Vittorio Gui** (1885–1975), Italian conductor and composer. In 1928, he founded the organization that developed into the Maggio Musicale (Florence). International appearances as opera conductor, especially in Britain. (Photo: Vaghi, Parma; signed 1935.)

60

61

60. Robert Heger (1886–1978), German conductor and composer. Active in numerous German cities and in London. (Photo: Residenz Atelier, Vienna.) **61. Siegmund von Hausegger** (1872–1948), Austrian conductor and composer. Active in various Austrian and German centers, especially Munich from 1922. (Photo: Elvira, Munich; Signed 1912.)

62

63

64

62. Joseph Hellmesberger (1828–1893), Austrian conductor. Conducted the concerts of the Gesellschaft der Musikfreunde (Vienna), 1851–59, and headed the Vienna conservatory. Own string quartet, 1849–91. (Photo signed 1870.) **63. Ferdinand Hellmesberger** (1863–1940), Austrian conductor, son of Joseph Hellmesberger. Conducted opera in Vienna, ballet in London, and spa orchestras in Marienbad, Carlsbad and elsewhere. **64. Johann Herbeck** (1831–1877), Austrian conductor and composer. Conducted the concerts of the Gesellschaft der Musikfreunde, 1859–70 and 1875–77. Director of the Vienna Court Opera, 1870–75.

65

66

65. Sir George Henschel (1850–1934), British conductor, composer and concert singer of German birth. Conducted Boston Symphony, 1881–84, and founded the London Symphony Concerts in 1886. (Photo: Elliott & Fry, London, ca. 1883; signed London, 1903.) **66. Alfred Hertz** (1872–1942), American conductor of German birth. At Metropolitan Opera, 1902–15, where he conducted the first non-Bayreuth *Parsifal* (1903) and the world premiere of Humperdinck's *Königskinder* (1910). Later, directed the San Francisco Symphony, 1915–30, and inaugurated the Hollywood Bowl concerts (1922). (Photo: Schieberth, Vienna; signed Vienna, 1930.) **67. Franz von Hoesslin** (1885–1946), German conductor. Active in numerous German cities.

67

68

69

68. **Wilhelm Jahn** (1834–1900), Moravian conductor. Was musical director of the Vienna Court Opera. (Photo: Fritz Luckhardt, Vienna; signed Vienna, 1891.) 69. **José Iturbi** (born 1895), Spanish conductor and pianist. Conducted the Rochester Philharmonic, 1936 ff. 70. **Willem van Hoogstraten** (1884–1965), Dutch conductor. Associate conductor of the N.Y. Philharmonic, 1923–25. Later, conductor of the Portland (Ore.) Symphony, 1925–27; the Mozarteum Orchestra (Salzburg), 1939–45; the Stuttgart Philharmonic from 1949.

70

71. **Otakar Jeremiáš** (1892–1962), Czech conductor and composer. First conductor of the Prague Radio Symphony, from 1929. Opera director of the National Theater, Prague, 1945–47. (Photo signed 1935.) **72. Karel Boleslav Jirák** (1891–1972), Czech conductor and composer. After holding several European posts, he taught in Chicago from 1947 to his death. (Photo: Drtikol & Pol, Prague, 1929; signed 1929.) **73. Sergey Jarov** (born 1896), Russian choral conductor. Leader of the Don Cossack Chorus. (Photo: Atelier Elite, Berlin; signed 1929.)

74

74. Hugo Jüngst (1853–1923), German choral conductor and composer. Founder-leader of the Dresden Male Choral Society. (Photo: Atelier Adèle, Dresden.) **75. Viktor Keldorfer** (1873–1959), Austrian choral conductor and composer. Chief conductor of the Vienna Männergesang-Verein, 1909–21; director of the Schubertbund, 1922–38 and 1945–54.

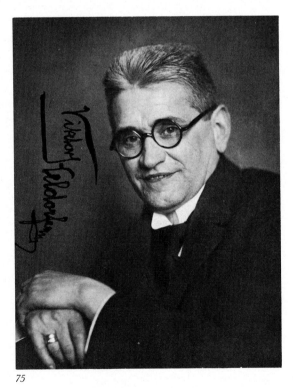

75

76

76 & 77. Herbert von Karajan (born 1908), Austrian conductor. Activity in Ulm, Aachen, Berlin (from 1941), Vienna, Milan (La Scala, from 1948), London, Bayreuth, Salzburg, ... Principal conductor of Berlin Philharmonic from 1955; director of Vienna State Opera, 1957–64. One of the most prominent twentieth-century conductors.

77

78

79

80

81

82

78. **Joseph Keilberth** (1908–1968), German conductor. Opera conductor in Karlsruhe, Dresden, Munich, Bayreuth. Music director of Bavarian State Opera (Munich) from 1959. (Photo: Liselotte Strelow, ca. 1954.) **79. Thor Johnson** (1913–1975), American conductor. Music director of the Cincinnati Symphony, 1947–67; director of Nashville Symphony, 1967–75. (Photo: Oggiano, N.Y.) **80. Hans Kindler** (1892–1949), Dutch conductor and cellist active in U.S. Conducted world premiere of Stravinsky's *Apollon Musagète* (Washington, D.C., 1928). Founder-leader of National Symphony, Washington, 1931–48. (Photo:

Underwood & Underwood, Washington, 1932.) **81. István Kertész** (1929–1973), German conductor of Hungarian birth. General music director at Cologne from 1964 to his death; principal conductor of the London Symphony, 1965–68. **82. Bruno Kittel** (1870–1948), German conductor. Founder of the Kittelscher Chor (choral society). In this group photographed at Bayreuth in 1931, Kittel is at the far right. The others, left to right, are "Spring" (no further information), Furtwängler (see nos. 46 & 47), "Tietjen" (perhaps Heinz Tiessen; see no. 177), Winifred Wagner and Toscanini (see nos. 175 & 176).

83

84

85

83. **Erich Kleiber** (1890–1956), Austrian conductor. Music director of the Berlin State Opera, 1923–34; at the Teatro Colón (Buenos Aires), 1937–49. Important activity at Covent Garden, 1950–53. **84. Hans Knappertsbusch** (1888–1965), German conductor. Director of Munich Opera, 1922–36; at Vienna State Opera, 1936–45. After war, back to Munich; at Bayreuth, 1951–57. **85. André Kostelanetz** (1901–1980), American conductor of Russian birth. Conductor with CBS radio from 1930; principal conductor of the N.Y. Philharmonic's promenade concerts.

86

86. Otto Klemperer (1885–1973), German conductor and composer. Director of the Kroll Opera (Berlin), 1927–31; conductor of the Los Angeles Philharmonic, 1933–39; principal conductor of the Philharmonia (London), 1955–72. A twentieth-century giant.

87

88

89

87. **Serge Koussevitzky** (1874–1951), American conductor of Russian birth. Formed own orchestra, 1909. After 1917, active in Berlin, Rome and Paris. Conductor of the Boston Symphony, 1924–49; founded the Berkshire Music Center at Tanglewood, 1940. 88. **Clemens Krauss** (1893–1954), Austrian conductor. Director of the Vienna State Opera, 1929–35; the Berlin State Opera, 1935–37; the Munich Opera, 1937–43. After the war, active in Vienna. (Photo: Arthur Benda, Vienna.) **89. Josef Krips** (1902–1974), Austrian conductor. Major musical figure in Vienna and Salzburg after World War II. Principal conductor of: the London Symphony, 1950–54; the Buffalo Philharmonic, 1954–63; and the San Francisco Symphony, 1963–70. (Photo signed Vienna, 1933.)

90

91

92

93

90. **Erich Leinsdorf** (born 1912), American conductor of Austrian birth. At Metropolitan Opera, 1937–43 and later; conducted Rochester Philharmonic, 1947–55; director of Boston Symphony, 1962–69. **91. Karl Krueger** (1894–1979), American conductor. Leader of: the Seattle Orchestra, 1926–32; the Kansas City Philharmonic, 1933–43; and the Detroit Symphony, 1943–49. (Photo ca. 1944.) **92. Adriano Lualdi** (1885–1971), Italian conductor and composer. Directed the conservatories of Naples, 1936–44, and Florence, 1947–56. (Photo: S. Stoppani, signed Milan, 1932.) **93. Hermann Levi** (1839–1900), German conductor. Leading conductor in Munich, 1872–90. One of the great Bayreuth conductors, he led the world premiere of *Parsifal* in 1882. (Photo: Adolf Halwas, Berlin.)

94

95

96

94. Sir Ernest MacMillan (1893–1973), Canadian conductor and composer. Principal of the Toronto Conservatory, 1926–42; conductor of the Toronto Symphony, 1931–56. (Photo: Everett Roseborough, Toronto.) **95. Lorin Maazel** (born 1930), American conductor. Began conducting at age 9. First American to conduct at Bayreuth, 1960. Music director of the Cleveland Orchestra from 1972. **96. Sir Charles Mackerras** (born 1925), Australian conductor. Began conducting opera in London, 1948. Also specialist in Baroque music.

97

98

97. Nikolay Malko (1883–1961), American conductor of Russian birth. Chief conductor of the Leningrad Philharmonic, 1926–29. In U.S. from 1940. (Photo signed Vienna, 1932). **98. Sir August Manns** (1825–1907), German conductor. One of the leaders of the Crystal Palace Band (London), 1855–1901. (Photo: Elliott & Fry, London.) **99. Luigi Mancinelli** (1848–1921), Italian conductor and composer. Chief conductor at Covent Garden, 1888–1905, and at the Metropolitan Opera, 1893–1903. The most important Italian conductor of the generation before Toscanini.

99

100

100 & 101. Gustav Mahler (1860–1911), Austrian conductor and composer. After activity in various German and Austro-Hungarian cities, he was at the Vienna Court Opera, 1897–1907 (one of the great periods in the history of that house); thereafter, with the Metropolitan Opera and the N.Y. Philharmonic. Great composer of symphonies and songs.

102

101

102. Jean Martinon (1910–1976), French conductor and composer. Major force in French music after World War II, and wide international activity. (Photo: A. C. K. Ware, London.) **103. Pietro Mascagni** (1863–1945), Italian composer and conductor. The celebrated composer of *Cavalleria Rusticana* (1890) was also a conductor of opera, especially of his own works, at La Scala and elsewhere.

103

104

105

106

104. Gino Marinuzzi (1882–1945), Italian conductor and composer. Conducted the world premiere of Puccini's *La Rondine* (Monte Carlo, 1917). Artistic director of the Chicago Opera, 1919–21. **105. Edoardo Mascheroni** (1859–1941), Italian conductor and composer. Chief conductor at La Scala, 1891–94; led the world premiere of Verdi's *Falstaff* (1893). (Photo: Witcomb, Buenos Aires; signed Buenos Aires, 1903.) **106. Gaetano Merola** (1881–1953), American conductor of Italian birth. In U.S. from 1899, conducted at both the Metropolitan Opera and the Manhattan Opera. General director of the San Francisco and Los Angeles Operas from 1923.

107

107. Willem Mengelberg (1871–1951), Dutch conductor. Led the Amsterdam Concert-gebouw Orchestra, 1895–1945, with many guest appearances elsewhere.

108. Yehudi Menuhin (born 1916), American violinist and conductor. A virtuoso from age 8, he has also conducted at music festivals in Bath, Windsor and Gstaad. **109. Zubin Mehta** (born 1936), Indian conductor. Conducting since the late 1950s, he was with the Montreal Symphony, 1960–67, and became music director of the Los Angeles Symphony in 1962. Director of the N.Y. Philharmonic from 1976. (Photo: Scavullo.)

109

108

110

110. **André Messager** (1853–1929), French composer and conductor. This outstanding operetta and ballet composer was music director of the Opéra-Comique (Paris), 1898–1903 and 1919–20, conducting the world premieres of Charpentier's *Louise* (1900) and Debussy's *Pelléas et Mélisande* (1902). (Photo: Underwood & Underwood.) **111. Joseph Messner** (1893–1969), Austrian conductor and composer. For many years, from 1926, led cathedral concerts during the Salzburg Festival. (Photo: Traub; signed Salzburg, 1935.)

111

112

113   *114*

52

115

112 & 114. Dimitri Mitropoulos (1896–1960),
American conductor of Greek birth. After conducting in Athens and Berlin, he led the Minneapolis
Symphony, 1937–49, and the N.Y. Philharmonic,
1949–58. (Photo 112: Paul Duckworth, N.Y. Photo
114: Susan Hoeller, N.Y.; signed 1943.) **113.
Bernardino Molinari** (1880–1952), Italian conductor. Artistic director of the Augusteo Orchestra
(Rome), 1912–43. (Photo signed Rome,
1932.) **115 & 116. Pierre Monteux** (1875–1964),
American conductor of French birth. Began
conducting at age 12. With Diaghilev, led the world
premieres of Stravinsky's *Petrushka* (1911) and *The
Rite of Spring* (1913), Ravel's *Daphnis et Chloé* (1912)
and Debussy's *Jeux* (1912). Also with Metropolitan
Opera, Boston Symphony and (1936–52) the San
Francisco Symphony. Founder-leader of the Orchestre Symphonique de Paris, 1929–38. (Photo
115: Mishkin, N.Y.)

116

117

118

119

117. Rudolf Moralt (1902–1958), German conductor. Chief conductor at Vienna State Opera, 1940–58. (Photo: Jos. Kaab; signed Vienna, 1934.) **118. Leopoldo Mugnone** (1858–1941), Italian conductor and composer. Conducted the world premieres of Mascagni's *Cavalleria Rusticana* (1890) and Puccini's *Tosca* (1900). **119. Felix Mottl** (1856–1911), Austrian conductor and composer. Conductor of opera and concerts at Karlsruhe, 1881–1903. Great Bayreuth conductor, from 1886. Director of Munich Opera, 1903–11. (Photo: Oscar Suck, Karlsruhe; signed Karlsruhe, 1895.)

121

120. Charles Münch (1891–1968), French conductor. After 15 years of activity in Paris, he became chief conductor of the Boston Symphony in 1948, remaining until 1962. (Photo: Meusy, Besançon.)
121. Carl Muck (1859–1940), German conductor. Music director of the Berlin Opera from 1908; also active in Boston and Hamburg. Greatest Wagner conductor of his time.

120

122

123

124

122. Arthur Nikisch (1855–1922), Austro-Hungarian conductor. Principal conductor of Leipzig Opera, 1879–89. Conductor of Boston Symphony, 1889–93. From 1895 to his death, he led both the Gewandhaus Orchestra (Leipzig) and the Berlin Philharmonic. One of the very great conductors. (Photo: J. C. Schaarwächter, Berlin; signed Leipzig, 1897.) **123. Siegfried Ochs** (1858–1929), German choral conductor and composer. Founder-leader of the Philharmonic Choir in Berlin. (Photo: Reichard & Lindner, Berlin; signed Berlin, 1910.) **124. Karl Münchinger** (born 1915), German conductor. Founder-leader of the Stuttgart Chamber Orchestra (1945), specializing in Bach.

125

125. Eugene Ormandy (born 1899), American conductor of Hungarian birth. Led Minneapolis Symphony, 1931–36. Music director of Philadelphia Orchestra, 1938–74, developing the sumptuous sound for which that orchestra was noted. (Photo: Adrian Siegel.)

126

127

128

126. Otakar Ostrčil (1879–1935), Czech conductor and composer. Active with various musical organizations in Prague, showing special concern for the proper performance of old and new Czech music. (Photo: Drtikol, Prague; signed Prague, 1928.)
127. Ettore Panizza (1875–1967), Argentinian conductor and composer. At Covent Garden, 1907–14 and 1924. At La Scala, 1921–29, 1930–32, 1946–48. At Metropolitan Opera, 1934–42. (Photo: A. Badodi, Milan; signed Vienna, 1933.) **128. Bernhard Paumgartner** (1887–1971), Austrian conductor and composer. Closely connected with the Salzburg Mozarteum and Festival. (Photo signed Salzburg, 1937.)

129

130

129. **Jonel Perlea** (1900–1970), Rumanian conductor and composer. Became music director of the Bucharest Opera in 1934. At Metropolitan Opera in 1949/50 season. Continued to work and teach in the U.S. (Photo: Bender, N.Y.) **130. Wilfrid Pelletier** (1896–1982), American conductor of Canadian birth. At Metropolitan Opera, 1917–49. Activity in Montreal culminated in a high cultural post in the Quebec government, 1961–70. (Photo: Raylee Jackson, N.Y.) **131. Emil Paur** (1855–1932), Austrian conductor and composer. Led Boston Symphony, 1893–98, and the Pittsburgh Symphony, 1904–10. (Photo: Aimé Dupont, N.Y.; signed 1904.)

131

133

132

132. Giorgio Polacco (1875–1960), Italian conductor. At the Metropolitan Opera, 1912–17. Principal conductor of the Chicago Civic Opera, 1922–30. (Photo: Mishkin, N.Y.; signed N.Y., 1915.) **133. Egon Pollak** (1879–1933), Czech conductor. Active in various German cities and (1915–17) with the Chicago Opera. (Photo signed Vienna, 1932.)

134

135

136

134-136. Fritz Reiner (1888–1963), American conductor of Hungarian birth. Principal conductor of the Cincinnati Symphony, 1922–31; then with the Pittsburgh Symphony, 1938–48; the Metropolitan Opera, 1948–53; and the Chicago Symphony from 1953. (Photos: Pictorial Parade.)

137

139

137. **Günther Ramin** (1898–1956), German choral conductor and composer. Directed major choral societies in Leipzig and Berlin from the 1920s to the 1950s. (Photo: C. Schäfer, Elberfeld, signed in Leipzig.)   138. **Sergey Rachmaninoff** (1873–1943), Russian pianist, composer and conductor. Well known for his concertos and other works, he also conducted opera at the Bolshoi (Moscow), 1904–06, but twice declined the post of permanent conductor of the Boston Symphony.   139. **Joseph Rosenstock** (born 1895), Polish conductor. Conducted opera in various German cities; led the Nippon Philharmonic (Tokyo), 1936–41; was music director of the N.Y. City Opera, 1948–55; later moved to the Cologne Opera. (Photo signed Wiesbaden, 1929.)

138

140

140. Sir Landon Ronald (1873–1938), English conductor and composer. Active in London, Berlin, Vienna, Leipzig and Amsterdam. (Photo: Bassano, London; signed London, 1925.)
141. Hans Richter (1843–1916), Austro-Hungarian conductor. From 1875, conducted the Vienna Philharmonic and at the Vienna Court Opera. Led the first entire *Ring* at Bayreuth, 1876, and was active at other music festivals. Conducted the Hallé Orchestra (Manchester), 1897–1911, and the London Symphony, 1904–11. At Covent Garden, 1904–11. One of the earliest internationally acclaimed conductors.

141

142. Artur Rodzinski (1892–1958), American conductor. Led the Los Angeles Philharmonic, 1929–33; the Cleveland Orchestra, 1933–43; the N.Y. Philharmonic, 1943–47; and the Chicago Symphony, 1947–48.

143

144

143. Max Rudolf (born 1902), American conductor of German birth. At Metropolitan Opera, 1945–58; music director of the Cincinnati Symphony, 1958–70. **144. Pedro Sanjuán** (1886–1976), Spanish conductor and composer. Organized the Havana Philharmonic, 1926, and conducted it, 1926–32 and 1939–42.

145

146 147

148

149

145. Sir Malcolm Sargent (1895–1967), English conductor. Principal conductor of the Hallé Orchestra (Manchester), 1939–42; of the Liverpool Philharmonic, 1942–48; of the BBC Symphony, 1950–57. Also important choral and operatic conductor, and Gilbert & Sullivan specialist. **146. Vassily Safonov** (1852–1918), Russian conductor and pianist. After decades of activity in Moscow, he led the N.Y. Philharmonic, 1906–09. (Photo: Mebius, Moscow; signed Vienna, 1904.) **147. Franz Salmhofer** (1900–1975), Austrian conductor and composer. Director of the Vienna State Opera,

1945–55, and Volksoper, 1955–63. (Photo: Hella Katz, Vienna; signed 1935.) **148. Fritz Scheel** (1852–1907), German conductor active in U.S. Founder-leader of the San Francisco Symphony, 1895–99, and the Philadelphia Orchestra, 1900–07. **149. Franz Schalk** (1863–1931), Austrian conductor. Director of Vienna Court (State) Opera, 1918–29, conducting the world premiere of Strauss's *Die Frau ohne Schatten* (1919). Also conducted at Covent Garden and the Metropolitan Opera. (Photo: Charles Scolik, Vienna.)

150

151

150. Max von Schillings (1868–1933), German
composer and conductor. Opera and concert conductor in Stuttgart, 1908–18; headed the Berlin
Opera, 1918–25. (Photo: Elvira, Munich,
1904.) **Paul Scheinpflug** (1875–1937), German
conductor and composer. After activity in several
German cities, he led the Dresden Philharmonic
from 1929 to 1933.

152

152. **Hans Schmidt-Isserstedt** (1900–1973), German conductor and composer. Founder-leader of the North German Radio Symphony (Hamburg), 1945–71, and principal conductor of the Stockholm Philharmonic, 1955–64. (Photo: Pictorial Parade.) **153. Hermann Scherchen** (1891–1966), German conductor. Varied activity in Germany and (from 1933) Switzerland. Internationally active after World War II. A champion of contemporary music. (Photo signed Vienna, 1937.)

153

154

154. Ernst von Schuch (1846–1914), Austrian conductor. Associated with the Dresden Opera from 1872 on, he conducted the world premieres of four Strauss operas: *Feuersnot* (1901), *Salome* (1905), *Elektra* (1909) and *Der Rosenkavalier* (1911). (Photo: Adèle, Dresden; signed 1903.) **155. Anton Seidl** (1850–1898), Austro-Hungarian conductor. After work at the Leipzig and Bremen Operas, he was at the Metropolitan Opera from 1885 on and led the N.Y. Philharmonic from 1891 on. Specialized in Wagner. (Photo: Falk, N.Y.)

155

157

156. Tullio Serafin (1878–1968), Italian conductor. Principal conductor at La Scala, 1909–14 and 1917–18 (conducted world premiere of Montemezzi's *L'Amore dei tre re,* 1913); at the Metropolitan Opera, 1924–34 (world premieres of Taylor's *The King's Henchman,* 1927, and *Peter Ibbetson,* 1931, of Gruenberg's *The Emperor Jones,* 1933, and of Hanson's *Merry Mount,* 1934). Continued conducting till 1962. (Photo signed Buenos Aires, 1920.) **157. Giulio Setti** (1869–1938), Italian conductor active in U.S. Associated with the Metropolitan Opera from 1911 to 1935. (Photo: Mishkin, N.Y.)

156

158

158 & 159. Sir Georg Solti (born 1912), British conductor of Hungarian birth. Music director of Bavarian State Opera (Munich), 1946–52; of Covent Garden, 1961–71; of the Chicago Symphony, from 1969; and of L'Orchestre de Paris from 1971. Principal conductor of the London Philharmonic from 1979. (Photo 158: Sedge LeBlang.)

160

160. Robert Shaw (born 1916), American conductor. Founder-leader of Robert Shaw Chorale, 1948–66. Conducted San Diego Symphony, 1953–57. Music director of Atlanta Symphony from 1967. **161. Fabien Sevitzky** (1891–1967), Russian conductor active in U.S. Founder-leader of the Philadelphia Chamber String Sinfonietta, 1925–37. Permanent conductor of the Indianapolis Symphony, 1937–55.

161

162

163

162. Carl Schuricht (1880–1967), German conductor and composer. Music director at Wiesbaden, 1911–44, then moved to Switzerland. (Photo: Daily Express, Manchester.) **163. William Steinberg** (1899–1978), American conductor of German birth. Music director at Frankfurt a/M, 1929–36. First conductor of the Palestine Orchestra (later Israel Philharmonic), 1936. Music director of the Buffalo Philharmonic, 1945–52, of the Pittsburgh Symphony, from 1952, and of the Boston Symphony, 1969–72.

164

165

164. Bernhard Stavenhagen (1862–1914), German pianist, conductor and composer. This virtuoso pupil of Liszt also conducted orchestras in Weimar, Munich and Geneva. (Photo: Krziwanek, Vienna; signed 1890.) **165. Fritz Stiedry** (1883–1968), American conductor of Austrian birth. Principal conductor of the Berlin State Opera, 1914–23; of the Berlin Municipal Opera, 1928–33. Regular conductor at the Metropolitan Opera, 1946–58. (Photo signed Vienna, 1926.)

166

166. Leopold Stokowski (1882–1977), American conductor of British birth. Vigorous leader of Philadelphia Orchestra, 1912–37; a champion of modern composers. Long subsequent career of guest appearances, youth concerts and orchestral appointments, including the Houston Symphony, 1955–60. (Photo 1934.)

167

168

167. Johann Strauss (1825–1899), Austrian composer and conductor. The "Waltz King" led his own world-famous orchestra, founded by his father, Johann, Sr. From 1863 to 1871, he was in charge of Viennese court ball music. **168. Eduard Strauss** (1835–1916), Austrian conductor and composer. Younger brother of Johann, he became co-director of the family orchestra with their brother Josef, then sole director from 1870. Eduard was in charge of the court ball music, 1872–1901, and also toured all over the world. (Photo: Pietzner, Vienna.) **169. Richard Strauss** (1864–1949), Austrian composer and conductor. This major composer of operas and symphonic works was also a great conductor in Meiningen, Munich, Weimar, Berlin and Vienna (co-director of State Opera with Schalk, 1919–24).

169

170

171

170. **Václav Talich** (1883–1961), Czech conductor. Principal conductor of the Czech Philharmonic (Prague), 1919–41, and head of opera at the National Theatre, Prague, 1935–44. Great interpreter of Czech composers. (Photo signed Prague, 1936.) **171 & 172. George Szell** (1897–1970), American conductor and composer of Hungarian birth. Began performing his own works at the piano at age 11, began conducting at age 16. After many posts in Europe, he led the Cleveland Orchestra from 1946 to 1970, and made international guest appearances. (Photo 171: 1940. Photo 172: London Stereoscopic Co., signed 1909.) **173. Igor Stravinsky** (1882–1971), Russian composer and conductor. One of the major twentieth-century composers, he often conducted his own works from 1915 on. (Photo: Lipnitzki, Paris, 1929.)

172

173

STUDIO LIPNITZKI
PARIS
1929

174

175

174. Eugen Szenkar (born 1891), Hungarian conductor. After many prestigious European assignments, he became permanent conductor of the Brazilian Symphony (Rio), 1939-50, and later became music director in Düsseldorf. (Photo: Feldscharek, Vienna; signed Vienna, 1930s.) **175 & 176. Arturo Toscanini** (1867-1957), Italian conductor. After his first conducting success in 1886, active in several Italian opera houses (conducted the world premieres of Leoncavallo's *I Pagliacci,* 1892, and Puccini's *La Bohème,* 1896); artistic director of La Scala, 1898-1908; artistic director of the Metropolitan Opera, 1908-15 (conducted world premiere of Puccini's *La Fanciulla del West,* 1910); back at La Scala, 1920-29 (world premiere of Puccini's *Turandot,* 1926); at Bayreuth, 1930-33; at Salzburg, 1934-37; leader of N.Y. Philharmonic, 1930-36; head of NBC Orchestra, 1937-54. Probably the most revered and influential of conductors. (Photo 175: R. Paganini, Milan, ca. 1930.)

177

177. Heinz Tiessen (1887–1971), German conductor and composer. Active as a conductor in Berlin, 1918–33. (Photo: Willott.) **178. Theodore Thomas** (1835–1905), American conductor of German birth. Associated with Brooklyn Philharmonic, 1862–91; headed his own orchestra by 1869; was music director of the 1876 Centennial Exposition in Philadelphia; conductor of N.Y. Philharmonic, 1877–91; thereafter, in Chicago as founder-leader of the Chicago Symphony. Pioneer popularizer of symphonic works in U.S. (Photo: Wm. M. Ruschhaupt, N.Y.)

178

179

179. **Donald Voorhees** (born 1903), American conductor. Very popular on radio, especially the Telephone Hour. (Photo: NBC.) **180. Henri Verbrugghen** (1873–1934), Belgian conductor and violinist. Conducted: Glasgow Choral Union, 1911–15; orchestras in Sydney (Australia), 1916–23; the Minneapolis Symphony, 1923–31.

180

181

181. Richard Wagner (1813–1883), German composer and conductor. Best known for his epoch-making music dramas, he was also a major conductor in many German cities, especially Dresden, 1843–48. (Photo: Emil Goetz, Lucerne.) **182. Siegfried Wagner** (1869–1930), German conductor and composer. Son of Richard, he conducted at Bayreuth from the 1890s and directed the festival there from 1906 until his death. (Photo: A. Pieperhoff, Bayreuth.)

182

183

184

185

183. Alfred Wallenstein (born 1898), American conductor. Music director of the Los Angeles Philharmonic, 1943–56. **184. Sir Henry J. Wood** (1869–1944), English conductor. Celebrated leader of promenade concerts in London from 1895 until his death. Also directed other orchestras and choral societies throughout England. In the photo he is seen with his first wife, the Russian soprano Olga Urusova, who died in 1909. **185. Hans Weisbach** (1885–1961), German conductor. Active in Düsseldorf, Leipzig, Vienna and Wuppertal. (Photo ca. 1939.)

Hans Winderstein

186

187

186. **Hans Winderstein** (1856–1925), German conductor. Led his own orchestra in Leipzig, 1896–1919. **187. Alexander Zemlinsky** (1871–1942), Austrian conductor and composer. Active as conductor of opera in Vienna, 1899–1911; Prague, 1911–27; and Berlin, 1927–30. (Photo: Adèle, Vienna.) **188. Bruno Walter** (1876–1962), German conductor. Active in Vienna and Munich,

1901–23 (conducted world premieres of Mahler's *Das Lied von der Erde,* 1911, and Ninth Symphony, 1912, and of Pfitzner's *Palestrina,* 1917). At Covent Garden, 1924–31; associate conductor of the Concertgebouw (Amsterdam), 1934–39; to U.S. from 1939, at the Metropolitan Opera and with various major orchestras. (Photo: C. Pietzner, Vienna, 1910; signed 1910.)

Frau Hermine Runz-Hubertrasser
zur freundlichen Erinnerung
Dezember 1910

Bruno Walter

188

189

190

191

189. Max Zenger (1837–1911), German conductor and composer. Active in Regensburg, Munich and Karlsruhe as conductor of operas, symphonic works and choral works. (Photo: A. Baumann, Munich, 1901.) **190. Hermann Zumpe** (1850–1903), German conductor and composer. Major international career, specializing in Wagner. (Photo: A. Baumann, Munich, ca. 1900.) **191. Carmen Studer-Weingartner** (dates unavailable), German conductor. Fifth wife of Felix Weingartner, she studied conducting with him and had a career of her own.

192

192. Felix Weingartner (1863–1942), Austrian conductor and composer. At Berlin Opera, 1891–98; at Vienna Court Opera, 1908–11; director of Vienna Philharmonic, 1908–27. Fabulous international career; one of the very great conductors.